HOWELL

Beginner's guide to

Guinea Pigs

Patricia Hutchinson

Editor
Dennis Kelsey-Wood

HOWELL BOOK HOUSE Inc.
230 Park Avenue
New York, N.Y. 10169

Library of Congress Cataloging-in-Publicat

j636.9
H97g

c.\

Hutchinson, Patricia.
  Howell beginner's guide to guinea pigs.

  Summary: Discusses the selection and care of guinea pigs including such aspects as housing, feeding, and exhibition. Also describes the different breeds and varieties.
  1. Guinea pigs as pets—Juvenile literature.
[1. Guinea pigs. 2. Pets] I. Kelsey-Wood, Dennis.
II. Title. III Title: Guinea pigs.
SF459.G9H88   1985   636'.93234   85-18452
ISBN 0-87605-930-2

Printed in Hong Kong through Bookbuilders Ltd

Photographs on pages 3, 11, 15, 22, 27, 29, 30, 31, 32, 33, 36, 37, 38, 39(1), 44 & 45
© Panther Photographic International

All Other Illustrations © Paradise Press

Contents

DEC '88

1 Introduction

The guinea-pig, or, to give its correct name, the cavy (*Cavia aperea porcellus*) and by which name it is referred to throughout this book, is the domesticated variety of the Wild or Peruvian Cavy (*C. a. tschudii*) which inhabits the mountain areas of Peru and Chile. Most other cavies of related genera are found in the grasslands of various regions of the South American continent.

It is known that the cavy was used, many centuries ago, by the Peruvian Indians for meat and sacrificial purposes, as well as being a household pet. Though the numbers are greatly reduced these days, this function still holds good with the more inaccessible tribes of the Andes. The cavies are not caged but are allowed to run freely around the homes of the Indians from whence they never venture too far. They were first introduced into Europe during the 16th century, by the returning Spanish Conquistadors and quickly found favor with the nobility and wealthier households as a family pet. The alternative name, guinea-pig, is thought to have arisen from a mistaken idea that the animals originated in Guinea, where the Spanish galleons called on the slave route from South America to Spain, whilst the shape of this little creature, together with its squeaking voice were both reminiscent of pigs – especially the young of the guinea-hog – which would have been very familiar to the traveller.

Cavies, like many other popular pets such as mice, rats, gerbils and hamsters, are members of the very large group of animals known as rodents; indeed, the order Rodentia, accounts for over half of all known mammals. The key to the success of this order of animals lies in their ability to adapt to almost every ecological niche and climate and, as a result, they are found on every continent in one form or another. Members of the family Caviidae, however, are indigenous only to South America.

The Cavy in the Wild

In the wild state the pelage (hair) of the cavy is short and either brown or gray, in varying shades, and is uniformly tipped with black. The coat is darker on the back, getting lighter as it progresses down the sides of the animal and may often be white on the chest and abdomen. It is from this simple combination that breeders, by careful selection, have produced the many patterns and colors of coat now seen.

Cavies, like most rodents, are social animals and live in small groups, families and loose colonies, which will number from four to ten or more. The group will be controlled by a dominant boar and will consist of several females and young cavies, including boars. As the group increases its numbers so fighting takes place between the males until one or more of the young boars will leave the group to set up its own family unit.

Wild (Peruvian) Cavy

Within the unit females also have an order of rank headed by a matriarch. Although cavies are not regarded as either climbers or jumpers, there is no doubt that the wild varieties are quite capable of doing both and one species in particular, the Rock Cavy, *Kerodon rupestris*, is quite adept at scampering up cliffs and trees, as well as making jumps of around one metre in height. Wild cavies make their homes in underground dens which they will either dig out for themselves or take over from other animals which may have abandoned them. As dusk approaches, the cavies will leave their home and tread familiar trails to forage for food which will consist of various vegetables and roots.

Some authorities state that the cavy is a diurnal animal (active during the day) and it may be that the degree of predation within an area dictates the timing of the cavies' feeding habits. The cavy has very limited defenses from predators and, therefore, relies chiefly on its fleetness of foot to escape. Because of this, it is a very alert animal which will scamper for cover at the slightest provocation.

Characteristics

The cavy displays many of the features which are regarded as typical rodent characteristics and a few which are not. The single feature which, with due consideration of other features, determines that a cavy is a rodent is its dentition.

Teeth. All rodents have two pairs of elongated chisel-like teeth called incisors – one pair in the upper jaw and one pair in the lower. No rodent has canine teeth, there being a large gap or diastema where these would normally be found. These incisors have open roots, as have the molars, and they grow continually throughout the animal's life. Their length is kept in check by the fact that they rub against each other when the animal is gnawing and feeding – which also serves to keep the teeth sharp. If injury or malformation should impair the alignment, this can have grave, often fatal, consequences as it restricts the cavy's ability to feed. In fact the teeth continue to grow, upwards and downwards, or outwards, and they have been known to grow into the upper or lower jaw. For this reason owners of cavies should always keep a careful watch on their animal's teeth. Needless to say any specimens that were born with faulty dentition should never be bred from, however outstanding they may be in all other respects.

Head. The cavy head is truncated (blunted) and the eyes are positioned at the side of the head which enables the cavy to see almost as well backwards as it can forwards. The upper lip is split at the front and the ears are typically small.

Body. The neck is thick and the body is cylindrical in shape, the cavy being a typical rodent in these respects. Body length ranges from 22 cm (8½ in.) to 34 cm (13 in.). The cavy is invariably described as having no tail, but this is

5

anatomically incorrect as the animal does have one, though it is greatly reduced and involuted (tightly curled) which gives the appearance of not having one. Weight 850–1,000 grams (30–35oz.). Body Temperature 39/40°C (102–104°F).

Feet and limbs. Legs are typically rodent, being short – the hind being longer than the front. The feet have four digits on the fore and three on the hind.

Communication. Cavies are capable of a wide range of high-pitched squeaks by which they communicate their mood of the moment. Like most rodents, they also make chattering noises by grinding their teeth in quick succession. Many rodents can hear ultra sonic sounds and it is probable this is true of the cavy.

General Remarks. The main difference between the cavy and most other rodents is that their young are precocial, which is to say they are born in an advanced stage of being able to move around and feed almost from the moment of birth. The adaptability of the cavy is illustrated by the fact that it shares with the mouse, rat, rabbit and hamster, the dubious distinction of being one of the foremost laboratory animals on account of its ability to thrive in very confined situations and also, being extremely docile, is very easy to handle. It may surprise many readers to know that the cavy is far hardier than is generally thought and has shown itself well able to endure sub-zero temperatures, always provided that it has access to a warm den with suitable bedding such as hay. In its native homelands there is, of course, a considerable temperature fluctuation between day and night. It should, however, be stressed that domestic cavies should not be subjected to extremes of temperature unless they have been very carefully acclimatized, and long-coated varieties will need even more consideration than the short-coated breeds.

Sadly, few zoological collections contain examples of wild cavy genera though many do keep related families such as the capybaras and agoutis. The nearest relative that you are likely to see in a zoo, is the Patagonian Cavy, or Mara, and you will find it a most interesting comparison to the small cavy you keep as a pet.

The foregoing description is but a quick resumé of these fascinating little animals in the wild and the following chapters will guide you through the care and selection of what is now one of the world's most endearing and popular pets.

The Classification of the Cavy and its Near Relatives

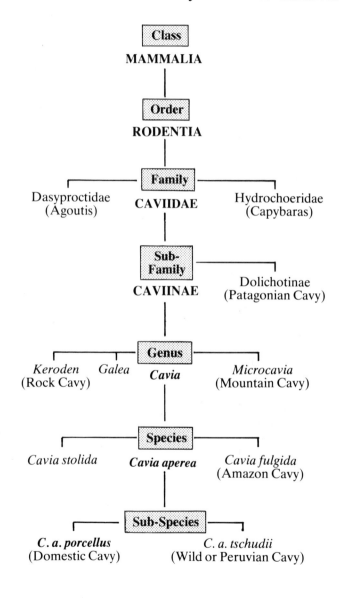

Class
MAMMALIA

Order
RODENTIA

Dasyproctidae
(Agoutis)
Family
CAVIIDAE
Hydrochoeridae
(Capybaras)

Sub-Family
CAVIINAE
Dolichotinae
(Patagonian Cavy)

Keroden
(Rock Cavy)
Galea
Genus
Cavia
Microcavia
(Mountain Cavy)

Cavia stolida
Species
Cavia aperea
Cavia fulgida
(Amazon Cavy)

C. a. porcellus
(Domestic Cavy)
Sub-Species
C. a. tschudii
(Wild or Peruvian Cavy)

2. Accommodation

General Considerations

The cavy is not an animal that demands elaborate or expensive accommodation, but what is provided should meet certain basic requirements to ensure that its occupants are warm, dry and have sufficient room in which to exercise. Should you live in a country that has considerable variation in seasonal climates, as, for example, in much of Western Europe or the Eastern United States, then it is advisable to keep your cavy in a shed or similar building to ensure a more even year-round temperature. This has the further advantage that you will be able to do routine cleaning even on days of bad weather.

Brick buildings are clearly ideal but if you use your garage then do so only if you are not using this for your car, as the fumes can prove lethal to your cavy. Likewise if a shed is used and shared with garden implements and such like then do ensure that no toxic liquids are stored there which might result in a build-up of lethal fumes.

An indoor building has the further advantage of giving you shelf space to store food, utensils and other needed items so that they are close at hand. A supply of electricity would be another advantage from your personal standpoint. The more straightforward and efficient it is to do routine work, the more you will enjoy keeping your cavies. It is important to see that the building has adequate ventilation, such as windows, and it is a good idea to have a double entry door, the outer being solid, and the inner one meshed; this enables you to leave the door open during fine weather and still keep the building dog and cat proof.

If the cavies must be housed outdoors, then they should be sited in the most protected area of your garden and not facing into the normal wind direction. It would be better if you could build a small carport-type structure to go over the actual hutch – of a height that would allow you some protection on wet days for feeding and routine cleaning, as well as affording the hutch that extra protection from inclement weather.

The Hutch

The actual hutch need only be quite simple, but it should be as roomy as

8

possible because cavies are far more active than is generally realized. Many of the hutches sold in pet shops are far too small and quite often the materials used for their construction are much too flimsy to stand up to long-term wear. Metal pens should be avoided. The floor area to accommodate a single cavy should not be less than 1,860 sq. cm (2 sq. ft) which would, in fact, be large enough for a pregnant sow to have, and rear, a litter to weaning age. Thereafter, 930 sq. cm (1 sq. ft) should be allowed for every additional cavy running in the same pen. It does not matter whether the hutch is oblong or square, though the former, in fact, makes better use of the area in that the cavies are easier to see and their running length for playing is greater. (The height should not be less than 38 cm (15 in.))

The front of the hutch should be covered with wire mesh of 1·3 cm (½ in.) gauge – otherwise mice will be able to get in, and the cavies may gnaw the mesh; cats will also be able to get their paws in to try and scratch the occupants. Assuming you have an oblong hutch, then the door can take up half the length of the hutch and it should be covered with the same mesh as the front. Cavies are liable to fall out of their hutch when the door is opened, or get their feet trapped when it is closed, so it is a good idea to have a small removable drop-board just inside the door. This need only be of hardboard about 7½ cm (3 in.) high, slotted into grooves to keep it in place.

A separated sleeping den is not necessary as this will reduce the available running space, though if you have a really large hutch then a den will be appreciated by the cavies who enjoy a little privacy and the feeling of security which this will provide. If there is a sleeping den then a separate door should be provided, again with a fitted drop-board. Cavies are very clean in their habits and will not foul their den to any degree, they are also

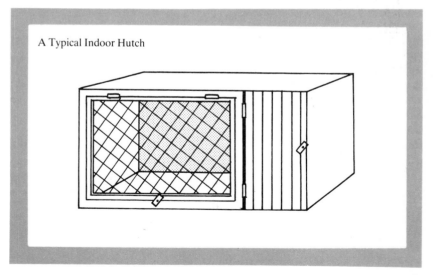

A Typical Indoor Hutch

odourless, therefore if their hutch ever smells it is a case of bad husbandry and not the cavies. If a sleeping den is not provided then give the animals a bit of privacy, either by making the door solid, or by tacking a piece of sacking or similar material over part of the mesh.

An indoor hutch can be made from less thick wood than one for outdoors but, even so, it should be substantial enough to withstand wear. Tongue and groove wood is best and, whatever wood is used, ensure that the floor has no gaps in it which might trap the cavy's small feet. Likewise, the sides and back should not have any gaps which might cause draughts. A stout-gauge plywood would, of course, obviate gaps. The hutch will not need treating with preservative, if it is sited indoors, and on no account should lead-based paints be used, especially inside the hutch, where the cavies could gnaw at it.

You will need a food receptacle and ideally this should be of the heavy earthenware type as plastic ones are easily picked up and turned over by the cavies who, at times, seem to do this for the sheer fun of it. Water is best placed in special bottles which are clipped on to the mesh and from which a tube supplies the cavy with fresh clean water. These are available at your local pet store. Contrary to some stories, cavies do need water which, depending on the weather, they drink in greater or smaller quantity.

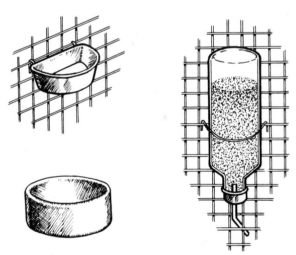

The hutch should be placed at a convenient height for you to see to the routine jobs without the discomfort of bending.

The Outdoor Hutch

Clearly the main difference between an outdoor hutch and an indoor one will be in respect of protection from the weather and there are many ways in which you can accomplish this. Firstly, the materials used must be substantial and the hutch will need to be on legs so that it is well clear of the

10

This charming group comprises a Cream, Coronet, Tortoiseshell and White, Abyssinian and a Strawberry Roan.

ground. To make it really cosy and if money permits, it can be double-skinned, that is to say, like a house with an outer and inner wall. Polystyrene or foam can be used as insulation between the walls. To prevent rain being swept in on very bad days a sheet of plexiglass (perspex) can be made to fit over the front (with due allowance being made for the protruding water bottle). The roof can be made to slope backwards and ideally should be covered with roofing felt or a similar material. The roof should be larger than the hutch to give some protection to the sides, back and front. The outside can be treated with wood preservative but this must be done before the cavies are accommodated to allow plenty of drying time. It is also more convenient if the hutch is placed on concrete, or paving slabs, from which droppings, sawdust, food and so forth can easily be swept up when cleaning. An outside hutch, like your home, will of course need regular inspection to see that it is kept in tip-top condition.

To keep the floor of the hutch clean, it can be lined with several thicknesses of newspaper on which clean, dry, wood-shavings, or coarse sawdust, are spread thickly. A good layer of soft hay should then be put on top, either in the den or in the screened-off sleeping area. When cleaning out, the whole lot can be pulled out on the paper lining and tipped straight into a bag or bin – having first removed the cavy into a temporary box.

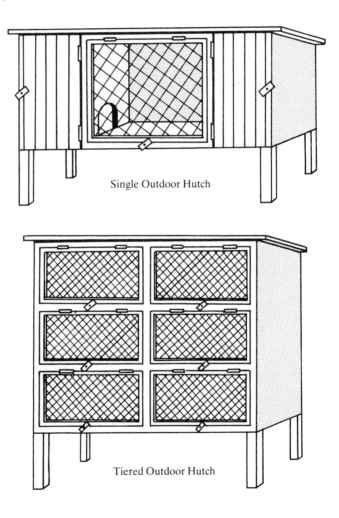

Single Outdoor Hutch

Tiered Outdoor Hutch

The Morant Hutch

During periods of warm weather you will want your cavy to enjoy the sunshine and one way of doing this is to build a Morant hutch which is a simple structure usually in the shape of a triangle, covered with wire mesh and which is covered with wood at one end in order to provide shade for the cavy. The major advantage of a Morant hutch is that it can be moved around the garden to provide fresh grass for the cavy and, at the same time, the cavy is secure from cats and dogs. Any enclosure suitably secured will be greatly enjoyed by cavies on nice days but always include in it somewhere for the cavy to scamper into or under if it is suddenly frightened.

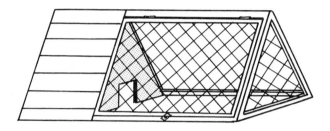

Enclosures

Whilst the hutches described are those that will be most practical for the average pet owner or breeder there is no reason why one should not add a touch of individuality. You may design a hutch in many ways that may give it a more natural look, or you may simply add a facade to the front.

If space and money permits the hutch might be placed in a walled or fenced enclosure and this adds further possibilities. Many zoos incorporate tunnels into their caviaries; small rocks and logs can give both refuge and places to explore. Other pets such as rabbits and even ducks can be seen sharing enclosures quite amicably with cavies. There really is no limit, providing always that you are aware of potential dangers such as cats or vermin and take adequate precautions against these. Certainly on warm days you will enjoy your pets more if they can be seen to play and explore within the confines of a secured area.

3. Feeding

One of the advantages of keeping cavies lies in the fact that they are very economical to feed. Most households throw away many leftovers that are quite acceptable cavy foods and, if local wild plants and grasses in your area are added to these, it leaves only a few items that must be purchased, in order to provide a stable all-the-year-round diet.

When you first obtain your cavy do check just what it has been feeding on and stick to this diet for a few days, after which you can gradually adjust this to suit your wishes. Cavies are very much creatures of habit and they do not take readily to sudden changes in diet which can quickly result in tummy upsets.

Grass

One food all cavies relish is grass, which can be fed to them throughout the summer months whilst it is available. Lawn mower clippings should not be given however, as they generate heat so quickly that it can cause serious

The Argenté Cavy

A Strawberry Roan Abyssinian Cavy

scouring. Cavies prefer long grass. If this is not collected in the garden, avoid picking it from places where it may have been fouled by dogs or car fumes. Obvious danger points are near fences, the trees of parks and on verges of busy roads.

Hay

Hay is needed, not only as bedding, but also to aid digestion. It is usually cheaper to buy by the bale than in small bags. The soft meadow hay is preferred and this will last a long while if stored in a dry place. Good hay will be greenish-yellow and smell fragrant – never musty – and you should pull a piece from the bale and see what the inner end looks like. Always be prepared to pay a little more for it to get the best as it really will pay dividends. Ideally, the hay should be about five or six months old; never feed fresh-cut hay. If you are unable to get mature hay then straw will suffice and this should be oat straw, which is bright yellow and has some feeding value.

15

...h is a pale yellow, not only has little food value but is ...barley straw, cannot be recommended. The spines found in ...eir hardness, may cause eye injuries to the cavies as they ...frisk about in the straw.

...orn is a valuable body-building food and examples are crushed oats, barley, maize, wheat and bran. They may be variously described as concentrates or cereals. It is possible, for convenience, to purchase bags of mixed corn from pet stores but this is often an expensive method simply because the cavies pick out those items they especially like and then leave the rest. The most popular cereal is crushed oats (cavies cannot eat whole oats) which can be fed as a mix with bran in the ratio of two parts oats to one part bran. This mix can be dampened with a little water to form a mash which is less wasteful. Uneaten mash must be discarded as it quickly turns sour, you will soon know just how much to prepare per meal. Barley should be fed more sparingly, as should maize, both of them having higher calorific value than oats. You will be able to experiment with various 'mash' combinations to establish which your cavy favors. Rabbit pellets are another form of cereal food though they are not as well liked by cavies nor are they a 'complete' food, as they are for Rabbits. They are concentrated, so need to be given with care otherwise you will finish up with overweight animals – availability of water at all times is essential when feeding pellets to cavies.

Vegetables

Being herbivorous, the cavy needs plenty of green foods which contain vitamin C; the cavy, like man, cannot manufacture this vital substance in its body (whereas a dog, for example, can). It should be pointed out that vitamin C deteriorates quickly when stored, so fresh vegetables are always recommended. The range of vegetables, roots and fruits that the cavy will enjoy is listed below:

Beetroot (Red Globe variety): Always a favorite with cavies, this is a first-class conditioner and body builder. Food content is high and vitamin C is present at about 3mg per ounce. The leaves are acid (oxalic) and should only be fed in small quantities. Beetroot will have the effect of coloring the cavy's urine (reddish).

Carrot: This has about the same vitamin C content as beetroot, and is another crop that is of high food value. Unwashed carrots will store longer than those already washed and bagged, but need washing just before being fed to your stock.

Turnips and Swedes: Very high vitamin C content (7mg per ounce) but otherwise of less food value, being mainly water and fibre and not appreciated by all cavies.

16

Sprouts, Cabbage and Broccoli: The vitamin C content is exceedingly high at 17/20mg per ounce. It is the leaves of sprouts that cavies enjoy, the actual sprout being ignored, whilst the thick stalks, when split, will also be relished by many cavies. Cabbage, but not the white variety, will be enjoyed though Spring-cabbage less so. The leaves of Broccoli, either the white or purple varieties, will be welcome.

Lettuce: Do not overfeed this for whilst being appreciated by cavies, too much can have an opiate effect due to the drug Laudanum found in it.

Celery: The outer leaves and stalks are appreciated. Vitamin C content 2mg per ounce.

Apples: These are much enjoyed though very low in vitamin C (1mg per ounce). They are ideal as tit-bits.

Various Fruits: Cavies enjoy a wide range of fruits which can include the trimmings in such fruits as strawberries, raspberries and blackberries. Grapes are taken readily. Use these as treats rather than basic diet.

Wild Plants

There is an extensive range of wild plants that will be greatly appreciated by all cavies and, of course, they help to keep your food bill down as well. It may well pay you to invest in a small identification book on the wild plants in your area so that you can familiarize yourself with just what they all look like. If you are at all uncertain about a given plant then the golden rule is 'if in doubt leave it out' until you have ascertained its value or otherwise.

Wild plants collected from under trees may have an acidic bitterness as a result of liquids exuded and dropped from the leaves and blossom of the tree; such plants should be avoided. Always feed wild plants as a mixture, as some may have a laxative effect which may be counteracted by another plant in the mixture. Remember that grass is your main plant and that all others are supplementary to it. As a guide to a number of the suitable – and poisonous plants – the accompanying table will be found most useful.

When to Feed

It is advisable to feed at least twice a day, and three times if possible. The first meal (morning) should comprise oats, or a dry cereal mix, with green-foods, and the main meal (evening) will comprise a mash together with their main greenfood dish. A midday meal would probably consist of some wild plants. Many people prefer to feed a mash in the evening as it will go off less quickly overnight than it would during the daytime. Keep the meals interesting by varying them and always remove any uneaten greens and mash before the cavy's next meal. If you find there are never any leftovers then increase the amounts, as the chances are you are underfeeding your stock. A final note is that toasted white or brown bread will be appreciated by the cavy both as a food and something on which to gnaw.

Some Edible Wild Plants

Bramble (*Rubus frutucosus*)
The young shoots are most readily eaten. Remove any leafy spines.

Chickweed (*Stellaria Media*)
Poor food value but contains useful trace element – copper. Not readily taken, but small quantities beneficial. Flowers are white.

Clovers
(*Trifolium pratense* and
T. repens – Red and White clovers)
Feed as mixture with other plants. Has good nutrient value.

Coltsfoot (*Tussilago farfara*)
Very palatable. Both the leaves and the yellow flowers are consumed.

Comfrey (*Symphtum officinale*)
Flowers white or pink. Nutritious as well as of astringent value.

Cow Parsley
(*Anthriscus sylvestris*)
Feed before the flowers start to appear in late summer. Nutritious and enjoyed by sows with young.

Dandelion (*Taraxacum officinale*)
This common plant will be enjoyed by stock though, due to its laxative properties, it should be fed mixed with other plants.

Dock (*Rumex acetosa*)
Feed in very small quantities – it has an astringent property so could be mixed with dandelion. Do not feed once the flower stalks appear; avoid spear-shaped leafed variety.

Ground Elder (Goutweed, Bishop's Weed)
(*Aegopodium podagraria*)
Has diuretic effect (increases kidney action resulting in excess urine) so feed sparingly, and before the flower stalks appear.

Groundsel (*Senecio vulgaris*)
Has laxative effect; often affected by white mould so check carefully.

Hawkweed (*Hieracium pilosella*)
Much enjoyed by most cavies.

Mallow (*Malva sylvestris*)
An excellent all-round plant with no bad side effects.

Nipplewort
(*Lapsana communis*)
Another excellent all-rounder. Similar flowers to dandelion.

Plantain
(*Plantago media* – Hoary;
P. lanceolata – Ribwort)
The broad-leaved is normally called plantain, and the long-leaved called ribwort. Both are excellent and contain vitamins and minerals lacking in other plants. May be fed to even the youngest cavies.

Sow (Milk) Thistle
(*Sonchus arvensis*)
Recommended for sow with young.

Shepherd's Purse
(*Capsella bursa-pastoris*)
A very popular plant for its astringent properties. May be kept as a dried plant for treating scouring. The whole plant can be fed.

Vetch (*Vicia sepium*)
These are wild peas and popular with many animal and bird keepers who believe they are especially beneficial for adding lustre to fur or feathers. Enjoyed by cavies.

Yarrow (*Achillea millefolium*)
Is called Milfoil by some people and has excellent tonic properties if given in small amounts.

Some Poisonous Plants (including those of dubious value)

Bracken
(*Pteridum aquilinum*)

Contains B1-destroying enzyme.

Buttercup
(*Ranunculus acris*) et al

This is safe when dried in hay but to be avoided when given mixed with grass. The odd plant will do no harm but try to weed out as much as possible from grass.

Bryony
(*Bryonia dioica* – white;
Tamus communis – black)

Both forms are very poisonous.

Charlock
(*Sinapsis arvensis*)

Poisonous in all its forms. Usually found growing with corn.

Deadly Nightshade
(*Atropa belladonna*)

Used in the preparation of the drug Hyoscymine.

Hemlock
(*Conium maculatum*)

Poisonous and even in minute doses has no beneficial properties for medicinal purposes. Easily confused with Hedge Parsley which is fed by some people to stock. Both are well left alone to avoid taking any risk.

Lily of the Valley
(*Convallaria majalis*)

Very lethal and used for making rodent poisons.

Privet
(*Ligustrum vulgare*)

Domestic farm stock are often ill and can die from this common shrub.

Scarlet Pimpernel
(*Anagallis arvensis*)

The whole of the family of Pimpernels should be avoided.

Ragwort
(*Senecio jacobaea*)

Due to delayed action, death from it may not be attributed to it.

Toadflax
(*Linaria vulgaris*)

Could be confused with small snapdragons.

Wild-beaked Parsley
(*Anthriscus sylvestris*)

To the above list can be added any plant that grows from a bulb such as daffodil or tulip, together with any plant that has been afflicted with white fungus or in any way looks to have been afflicted with any other disease.

4. Breeding

Most cavy owners will, sooner or later, wish to breed from their stock and this will be found to be most rewarding. There is a special excitement about your cavy's first litter and, no doubt, the whole family will share in this and the joy of seeing the first tiny little piglets scampering around the hutch within hours of their birth.

Whilst cavies are not difficult to breed, they could not be considered easy or prolific breeders as can be many other rodents; but that is not to say that, with due care, you should encounter any special problems.

Considerations

Before any breeding operations are undertaken, you should consider one or two important points. Firstly, if your stock is a 'mixed bag' purchased as pets from your local store, then the resulting litters will be similar and the potential market for them will be much smaller than if you acquired pure-bred animals. Later you may wish to exhibit your cavies so, again, the stock will need to be pure and this will, in any case, increase your chances of selling it even if you do not exhibit. Such animals may cost a little more as you enter the hobby but will be a far better investment in the long run and will be found to be more interesting as a breeding proposition.

If you do decide to purchase a breed-type, then a breeding trio is recommended. Study the varieties at the end of this book and, if it is your first cavy venture, select one of the more popular, short-coated, varieties with which to gain experience before tackling those requiring special grooming.

Never breed from immature animals and, on no account, from stock that is in any way ill, unfit or shows a deformity of any kind.

Essential Facts

Cavies, unlike many other rodents, do not give birth to high numbers of young, one to four being typical, though larger numbers are not unknown. The gestation period is very long, being sixty to seventy-two days, sixty-five to seventy being usual, but, at the end of this, the young are born fully furred and able to move around and feed within hours of birth. The young will be suckled for two to four weeks, the latter being usual. The female is able to breed throughout the year, though spring to autumn is favored by most owners, and the oestrus cycle is normally sixteen to nineteen days; between cycles, the female will be about another sixteen days but this can vary considerably within different individuals.

Breeding Age

A boar is capable of successful mating from a very early age, ten weeks would be normal – earlier than this it is more likely he will go through the actions of mating without actual fertilization taking place. The female is also capable of conceiving at an early age but it is unwise to allow her to do so at less than five months. Conversely, a sow that has not been mated by the age of twelve months is best left as a non-breeder, as the pelvic girdle and ligaments may have become rigid and could cause complications.

The Mating and Birth

The boar should be placed in with the sow (or up to four sows as the case may be) and, provided the sow is in season, activity will soon take place. The boar will be seen to chase the sow around and there will be plenty of squealing going on. On no account should two boars ever be placed together as fighting will ensue and this can be very bitter with substantial damage being inflicted to one or other, or even both.

The advantage of running a boar with two or more sows is that this reduces the risk of you being disappointed should one of the sows not be prepared to mate. It is unlikely that you will see the actual mating take place and the first signs of success will be the sow showing obvious signs of pregnancy in the region of the uterus. By the fiftieth day the movements of the young within the sow will be apparent. At this time, try to avoid lifting the sow, whose weight will increase rapidly up to the time the young are born, and when you do have to pick her up make sure that the full weight of her abdomen is on the palm of your hand.

The question of whether or not the boar should be left with the sow or whether, if more than one sow is 'in pig', they should be left together, is one which you will have to decide and the possibilities are as follows:

(a) If only one sow is involved, then the boar can safely be left with her until shortly before she gives birth. He is safe with her even after the young are born as only rarely have boars been known to injure babies – usually they are ideal fathers. However, once the young are born, the female can immediately mate again and this is most likely to happen unless the male is removed. In the general excitement that accompanies mating, the young may be trampled upon or startled and thus injure themselves. A sow should never be allowed to be in pig whilst she is still nursing infants.

(b) If a number of sows are in pig together they may be left to litter together, but the problems are (1) that babies of the first litter to be born will be fussed

This Coronet Cavy will need extra grooming – but it will be worth the effort.

over by the other sows and this may excite them to the point of aborting their own litter and possibly dying in the process; (2) that babies will go to any nursing mother – and she will feed them, so that you have difficulty in keeping accurate records of who is who, and one of the sows may be overtaxed by having to cope with more than her share of youngsters!

(c) The pregnant mother may be removed, prior to giving birth, into her own pen to enjoy total privacy. This is, in the author's opinion, much the most desirable method as the risks of loss are minimal. The one word of caution is that this removal from her familiar surroundings and company can create a feeling of stress that could prompt her to abort. This is, however, overcome by placing the boar with her for a few days until she has become accustomed to the new surroundings.

Post-natal Care

Although the sow has only two milk glands, she is well able to cope with

22

four, or even more, youngsters as these seem to take their turn at feeding. If only one baby is born, then it will feed from the same teat and the other gland will dry up within a few days.

A dish of bread and milk, given daily in a clean pot, will be appreciated by mother and infants – especially if the litter is a large one. Should you have to hand-feed the babies for any reason, then one of the proprietary brands of milk for dogs, cats and pets should be mixed with warm milk to a runny consistency and given through an eye dropper every two hours until the baby is able to eat from the dish unaided. Hand-reared youngsters will, of course, have to be given hay and fresh greens, preferably grass, to supplement their diet.

When the babies are about four weeks old, they will need to be sexed and the boars removed – the sows can be left with their mother. Young boars can be left together for another few weeks, provided they do not have anything put into their hutch which has been near a sow, or otherwise this will induce fighting. Once they have reached seven weeks old, they should be separated and never again placed with other boars. Sows are quite safe with each other, only occasionally does one find a bully, in which case she should be removed until such times as a boar is run with the sows – he is very much in charge and does not permit such practices.

Breeding Age Limits

The upper breeding age of a sow will usually be about three years, whilst that of a boar will be longer – around four to five years. Matings of older animals are, of course, possible, those quoted being the average. You may expect your cavies to live to an age of six years though, here again, individuals of nine and ten have been recorded. Finally, you are not advised to allow sows to have more than three litters per year, if they are to remain in hard, fit condition, and most breeders rest their stock over the winter months, say from mid or late November to the end of January.

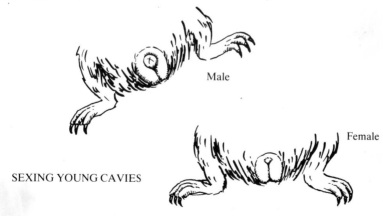

Male

Female

SEXING YOUNG CAVIES

5. General Management & First Aid

The essence of all good animal husbandry lies in attention to hygiene and regular and balanced diet. Given these two factors, illness, or the risk of it, will be substantially reduced. As has already been mentioned, cavies are, by nature, very shy creatures and, if you wish to get the best out of them, this will entail regular handling. The cavy has a heavy and pendulous body in relation to its limbs and, therefore, needs ample support when lifted. They have soft ribs which, if held tightly, will cause them to wriggle and they may jump from your hands doing an injury to themselves when landing.

It is most important that young children are both supervised and instructed on the correct way to pick up their pet. Slide your hand, palm upwards, underneath its tummy with your first and second fingers passing between its hind legs – which will thus be hanging over your fingers and so be unable to get leverage for jumping. The stomach is then supported by your palm and the cavy's front legs will rest on your wrist. By placing your other hand over its shoulders the cavy is now fully secure and will soon become accustomed to being lifted in this manner.

Should a cavy jump, or fall, from any height – even as low as 20cm (8in.) – it will almost invariably land on its nose possibly ending up with a cut mouth and broken teeth or, if landing on its feet, perhaps strain its muscles or break a limb. Broken teeth will, of course, grow again and normally these should be evened off with nail clippers so that eating is no problem. If knocked out altogether, food will have to be grated until the teeth start to re-appear.

Bathing

Under normal conditions the well kept cavy will not need bathing. However, certain breeds may benefit from such, especially if being exhibited. Cavies do not appear to mind being bathed provided they are handled with care. It is best to use a washing-up bowl which has been half filled with warm water. Do ensure that it is not too hot. Have a towel ready on the draining board on which to place the cavy during water changes. Lower the cavy, rump first, until it is covered to about its midriff and gently saturate its coat. Rub a hair shampoo into a lather and, if the cavy is really greasy, add a little washing-up liquid. On no account should you get water into the cavy's eyes or ears so the head is best wiped with a damp cloth afterwards. Rinse, and then repeat the shampooing and finally rinse until all traces of soap are gone. Hand towel the cavy as dry as possible and finish with a hand dryer if you have one. Should the weather be on the cold side, then keep the cavy indoors overnight in a suitable box; but if it is warm outdoors, the cavy can safely be returned to its hutch where you can place extra hay for it to snuggle into.

Compaction of the Rectum

When boars start to age, one sometimes finds that the droppings compact into a large mass and will have to be removed. Vaseline will soften the lump if smeared around the edges of it. Removal is awkward and painful for the animal as the testes are stretched due to the compaction. It is also rather a smelly operation. Once cleared, place more vaseline around the anus and remove any build-up daily.

Fighting

Any wounds can be treated with a salt water solution in the same strength as for eyes, and dusted with B.F.I. or similar powder which you are advised to have on hand for just such emergencies.

Abcesses sometimes occur, usually in the neck area, and will become quite large before bursting. Once this has happened, wash with saline solution and clear as much pus away as possible each day. Clean out the hutch daily until the wound has cleared up. Never treat cavies with anti-biotics as they find them toxic and often die after these have been administered.

Lice

If a cavy has lice these are of a kind which is not transmitted to humans and which lives off the skin debris so is usually no problem, unless you are exhibiting your cavy. As many louse preparations sold for dogs and cats are unsuitable for cavies you should contact your veterinarian for a suitable product such as *Alugan* spray.

One mite that can cause great discomfort and even death (due to stress) is called Sellnick, which is a type of Sarcoptic mange. Bald red patches occur on the skin which irritate the animal and it is akin to scabies in humans. Other cavies can become infected with it (but not humans), therefore it must be treated as soon as it is evident.

The cavy will need dipping in *Alugan* solution until it is soaked. The solution must not be rinsed off but towelled dry and the process repeated about ten days later. Consult your veterinarian regarding the quantity to use.

Mouth Scabs

Sometimes a scab or crust will form at the corner of the mouth and steadily grow larger. What causes this is not known and the treatment is an application of vaseline in order to soften it. If it persists, however, consult your veterinarian for some *Panolog* or similar ointment.

Scouring (Diarrhea)

If the animal seems otherwise well, then it can be assumed this is caused by too much greenfood being fed when the animal is not used to it. Feed only dry food and water for the time it takes to see droppings back to normal – put a vitamin C tablet in the water. If, however, the animal is clearly unwell then it is probably enteritis which is a much more serious condition. The cavy should be isolated straight away, all bedding destroyed and the entire hutch thoroughly cleaned. Only water should be available, no food, and the veterinarian should be consulted immediately. It is usually associated with poor hygiene, so double-check that all feeder pots are clean and that no droppings or stale food are left lying around.

The Rex Cavy – one of the newer varieties which has a distinctive coat texture.

A Brindle Abyssinian Cavy is a popular choice with children.

Toenails

These can sometimes grow too long and start to curl into the foot. They should be trimmed regularly if this happens. Do not cut too much at a time lest you cut into the 'quick' which will then start to bleed. Should this happen, dip the nail into french chalk or baby talcum powder and the bleeding will soon stop.

Eye Injuries

If the eye becomes opaque it should be treated twice a day with a soothing eye ointment which will usually clear up within ten days. Sore or runny eyes often clear up if bathed in a solution of salt (1 teaspoon) and water (1 pint boiled and cooled). If the eye is swollen there may be a hay seed or husk somewhere in the eyelid and, if you cannot retrieve it by gently pulling the lid down, put eye ointment in and this often helps the seed to slide out sufficiently for you to remove it.

How to Select a Sound Cavy

Points to Look For	Avoid
1. *Eyes* should be bold, bright and clear.	Any that have small, runny or opaque-looking eyes.
2. *Ears* should be slightly drooping and large. The color should match the body.	Any that are very small and crinkled or are cut or do not blend in with the body color. These will not be important points in a pet cavy.
3. *Nose* should be clean. *Teeth:* One pair of incisors in upper jaw which overlap and just touch the pair in the lower jaw.	Any with runny or blocked nose, or with missing, deformed or damaged front teeth.
4. *Coat* should appear sleek with good lustre, soft and silky (see 4b).	Any that show signs of bald patches, scurf, mites, harshness or look dishevelled.
4b. *An Abyssinian cavy coat* should be harsh and the rosettes deep with definite pin-point centres. The ridges should be stiff and upright.	Any with soft coats or flat ridges. However, this would only apply to a potential show animal.
5. *Feet* should be inspected to ensure they are supple and well-formed.	Any which show a sign of injury or malformation.
6. *Body* should be supple and pendulous, yet firm.	Any which lack good substance.
7. *Rump* the anus should be clean.	Any which appear bony or have loose droppings stuck to their anus.
8. *General.* The cavy should be alert, active and giving the impression of being very fit.	Any that sit hunched in a corner or show disability or are housed in unhygienic conditions.

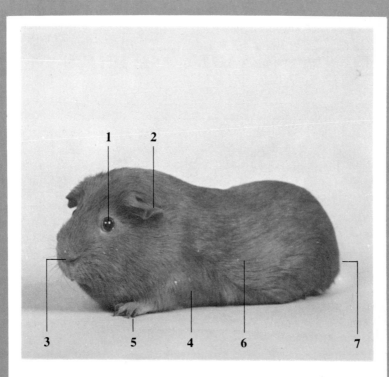

THE POINTS OF A CAVY

1. Eyes
2. Ears
3. Nose
4. Coat
5. Feet
6. Body
7. Rump

6. Breeds and Varieties

Cavies sold in pet shops are usually cross-breeds and it is not generally appreciated just how many different varieties have been developed over the years and are now bred for exhibition purposes. Many specialist clubs exist the world over in order to cater for the cavy fancier, to organize shows and generally promote the hobby.

Cute aren't they? This pair are just six weeks old.

Cavies are very inquisitive animals and
enjoy exploring – providing they can find
somewhere to hide if startled. This quartet
are obviously quite happy.

If you are about to purchase your first cavy it is strongly recommended that you visit one or more shows in your area and become familiar, not only with the many varieties, but also with the specialist breeders of them. During the warmer months, these shows are often held in conjunction with agricultural shows, and in the winter usually in local church halls, or similar places, and are advertized in the local press. Cavies are divided into two main groups, these being the Self Varieties and the Non-Self Varieties. The Self group are all smooth, short-coated cavies and, as their name implies, are of a single uniform color all over. The Non-Selfs comprise a number of varieties with a range of coat length and type. We shall look first at the former group.

The Self Varieties

Within this group color is of vital importance, accounting for nearly a third of the points allocated in a show animal. It is desired, though seldom achieved, that the coat color be consistent from the hair-tip to skin. The texture should be silky and in no way coarse. 'Type', which is the body and head shape, is also of great importance within the Selfs. Ideally, the head should be blunt, broad and 'bold'. The sow is generally the better in this respect. The body is square and cobby, with the shoulders broad and deep. The colors available are as follows:

Self Black
Probably the nearest to the 'ideal' Self cavy. At shows, competition in this color is always very fierce and the standard is such that the Self Blacks win more Best in Show awards than any other variety. The color must be a deep lustrous lack.

A fine show winning Black Cavy

The Self White Cavy

Self Cream
It is required that the color be pale and the under-color match this. There are both light and dark creams, and maintaining a consistency of color can be a major problem as breeding light to light or dark to dark is not to be recommended. Eyes are a ruby color.

Self White
This is another very popular color and specimens may have either pink or black eyes. A wide variety of whites will be found. Under-color is not a problem in this variety.

Self Beige
Type is usually not as good as in the previous colors. Eyes are pink. A medium-beige is normally preferred. Litters contain numerous shades and skill is required to select those most suitable. Youngsters are born dark, and lighten with maturity.

Self Golden
The color should be likened to a 'Golden Guinea' which means not too brassy or red. There should be no suggestion of yellow. Eyes are pink and the feet, ears and nails should match the body color which is often difficult in this variety.

Self Lilac
A difficult color to explain. It should be more akin to gray than to fawn. Eyes pink. Some are mistaken for beige, so seeing good examples is the way to register the color in one's mind.

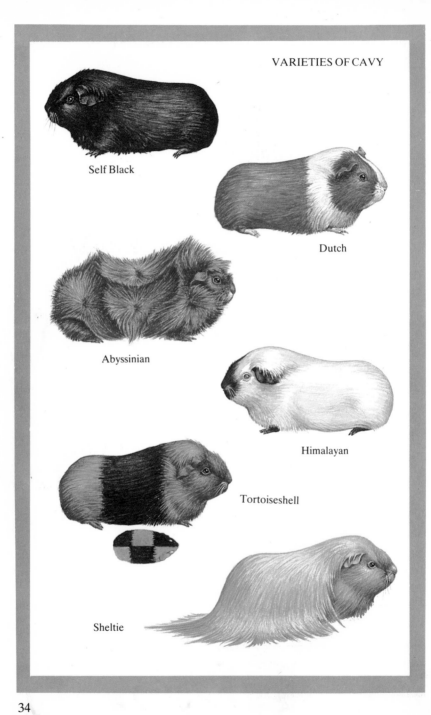

VARIETIES OF CAVY

Self Black

Dutch

Abyssinian

Himalayan

Tortoiseshell

Sheltie

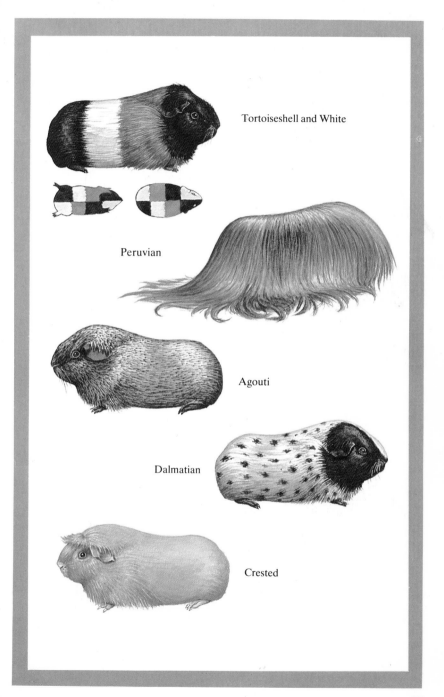

Tortoiseshell and White

Peruvian

Agouti

Dalmatian

Crested

Self Red
Once much more popular, it should be rich and dark – like mahogany. Eyes are ruby. It can be a difficult variety to succeed with, which might account for its loss of popularity. Youngsters may go from dark to light and back to dark. They may have white hair-tips which they lose with maturity to become excellent examples. Type is not as good as in other colors.

Self Chocolate
One of the oldest of the Selfs, this color is not so widely kept these days – more's the pity as it has possibly the finest hair texture of all the Selfs. Ears and feet should match the body color. Eyes are ruby.

The Non-Self Varieties

This group is represented by a number of varieties having varying coat lengths and color markings together with all of the more 'exotic' cavies.

The Abyssinian
Probably the most popular of this group, it is recognized by its numerous rosettes and ridges. It is a very active cavy and the only variety that is inclined to bite if mishandled. It is nevertheless well recommended for the beginner. It can be obtained in many color varieties such as Black, Red or White as well as in mixed forms such as Brindle, Roan or Tortoiseshell. More unusual are the Agouti and Himalayan marked specimens. The coat should be as rough or bristly as possible – the only cavy with this requirement.

The Abyssinian Cavy

An example of the Tortoiseshell and White Cavy

The Agouti
These are found in various colors, Golden and Silver being the most popular. They are short-coated and the ticking, which gives the characteristic appearance to the coat, is confined to the hair-tips. An Agouti should have evenness of ticking.

The Dutch
In rabbits this is a very popular variety, but it has not achieved the same success in cavies. Ideally, the area of color should exceed that of the white. Red is the most popular color followed by Black; other colors include Chocolate, as well as Golden, and Silver Agoutis. Where the color joins the white there should be as clean a line as possible and evenness of markings, for example on the legs, is very desirable in the show animal.

The Tortoiseshell and White
If you are the sort of person who likes a *real* challenge then this variety is tailor-made for you. The distinctive patchwork of red, white and black must be in sequence up one side of the body and in another sequence down the other side. Without doubt, a most beautiful cavy, but it is so difficult to produce a good one that they have earned the nickname 'the heartbreak' variety. A specimen coming anywhere near the standard can be shown, and one that actually excels is almost unheard of. They are, in many ways, a 'hit and miss' cavy in that it is almost a matter of luck whether or not you get one that is reasonably marked.

A fine pair of Self Cream Cavies

A young long-haired cavy makes
an attractive pet.

The Himalayan

This cavy has an all-white body with dark-colored extremities – as seen in the Siamese cat. There are both Black and Chocolate varieties. The Chocolate should be of the *milk* color not the plain as this would cause confusion over whether it was a good example of Chocolate or a poor Black. The challenge comes in that, as one improves the dark points, the coat tends to lose its white color and *vice versa*.

The Peruvian

This very long-coated cavy is not recommended for the beginner. The coat can grow to 50cm (20in.) and requires considerable time spent in grooming it. Very much a show cavy, it is the sort you either love or hate.

The Sheltie

This is another long-coated variety that is gaining popularity very rapidly. It was developed from the Peruvian and was accepted as a breed in the UK in 1973. The head is free of long hair, giving the cavy a very appealing look. Not as difficult to maintain as the Peruvian it is nevertheless not recommended for beginners.

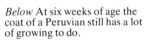

Below At six weeks of age the coat of a Peruvian still has a lot of growing to do.

Above Is it a wig? No, this is the Peruvian adult and that long coat means a great deal of grooming for someone!

A rare photograph of a pair of
Dalmatian Cavies.

The Dalmatian
As the name implies this is a white cavy which has black or gray spotting. It is
a mutation of the Self Black and is gaining rapid popularity. It is, of course,
smooth-coated.

The Roan
A smooth-haired variety having an even mixture of black and white hairs.
There should be no tendency towards patchiness. Developed from Blue
Roan Abyssinian × Self Black.

The Crested
This is another cavy that is gaining popularity. It has a short smooth coat and uniform color and sports a crest or rosette between the ears and eyes. Because of this rosette it cannot be called a Self, all of which are totally smooth. In England, the crest may be the same color as the body, but in the USA the crest is white on a contrasting body color. A number of color varieties are available and Agouti and Himalayan marked examples are now being developed.

Rare Varieties

Apart from the varieties already mentioned, there are a number of others which, even if they have official standards, are classed as Rare.

The Smooth Brindle
Another smooth-coated cavy, whose coat should be an even mixture of red and black.

The Tortoiseshell
A very old breed, it remains in the Rare Varieties group due to its relative scarcity. The color should be a combination of black and red patches in opposition – as seen in the Tortoiseshell and White but, of course, there is no white on the Tortoiseshell variety.

The Bi-colored
The Bi-colored cavy requirements are the same as for the Tortoiseshell in that the colors are in opposition. They can combine any two colors other than black and red; usually they are cream and black, red and white or chocolate and cream.

The Saffron
These are the nearest thing to a yellow cavy and produced from Self Goldens.

Others
Breeders are always experimenting in order to establish new types and the following are some of the varieties that are being established.

Sable; Harlequin; Strawberry Roan; Dark-eyed Golden; Cream Dutch; Lemon Agoutis; Rex; Argenté.

7. Exhibition

One very quick way to find out if the cavies you have bred are as good as you think they are is to exhibit or show them. This aspect of the hobby has much to recommend it for you not only have the possible thrill of winning, but also the chance of meeting other fanciers. Do not let the fact that you are a beginner put you off, as many a novice has won the very first time out. Obviously the experienced breeders will have a better chance, but even they were beginners once. There are many breeders who accept they will never win top awards, yet are regular exhibitors simply because they enjoy the friendly atmosphere and the company of those who share the same interests.

The Sheltie — an excellent show cavy.

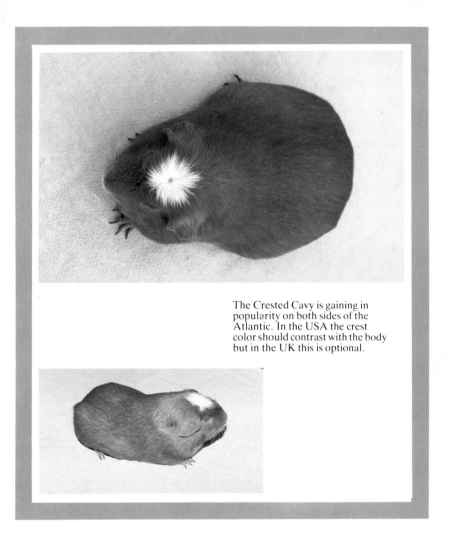

The Crested Cavy is gaining in popularity on both sides of the Atlantic. In the USA the crest color should contrast with the body but in the UK this is optional.

Another fact not always appreciated is that, whilst shows are all about pure-bred cavies, nevertheless, many clubs include in their schedules a class for pets which may be either cross-bred or pure-bred cavies – the latter for those that would normally not be good enough to enter the specialty classes. There are classes for novices (the definition of which may be that either the cavy or the owner has never won a first prize), juvenile classes for the younger exhibitors and breeders' classes for those showing the cavies they have bred. Space does not permit us to look at all the rules and classes but, as has been shown, every care is taken to make competition fair and to encourage all ages to take part.

You may well have visited a few shows before you purchased your own stock, but now you will visit them in order to see just what is entailed in showing. The exhibitors will always welcome newcomers and give you their advice.

The show cavy does, of course, require more attention to its appearance; this will entail careful grooming to remove guard hairs in the Self breeds, as well as being bathed a few days before the show. The cavy will need to be used to being handled by the judges and sitting still on the show-table, both of which will mean many practice sessions in your home beforehand. A

THE CORRECT METHOD
OF HANDLING A CAVY

Note that the pendulous body is supported whilst the cavy is secured with the other hand.

The positioning of the fingers is indicated below. This method provides support whilst not giving the cavy any leverage for jumping out of your hand.

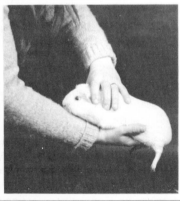

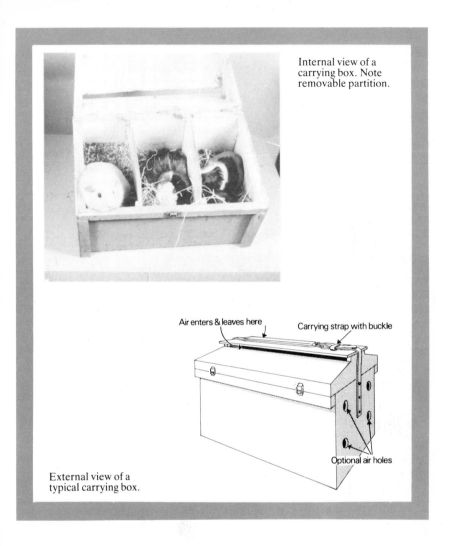

Internal view of a carrying box. Note removable partition.

Air enters & leaves here

Carrying strap with buckle

Optional air holes

External view of a typical carrying box.

proper carrying box will be required to transport your cavy to the show and you will need to take whatever grooming and personal items that you may require during the course of a day spent at the show.

Schedules and entry forms are obtainable from the secretary who will also give you advice on how to enter should you be unsure on certain points. You are clearly advised to join a local club and, in this way, the members will guide you on what you must and must not do. Your local information bureau may be able to supply the address of societies in your area but failing this look out for adverts of forthcoming shows in your local press.

A beautiful Self Black Cavy

The Peruvian Cavy

An Abyssinian Cavy
with his Agouti
marked friend.

The Self
Lilac Cavy

47

The Cavy at a Glance

Scientific Name	*Cavia aperea porcellus*
Size	22–34 cm (8½–13½ in.)
Weight	850–1000 grams (30–35 oz.)
Longevity (average)	5–7 years
Dental Formula	$\dfrac{1\ 0\ 1\ 0\ 3}{1\ 0\ 1\ 0\ 3} = \frac{1}{2}$ jaw = total 20
Rectal Temperature	39–40°C (102–104°F)
Adult Pulse Rate (per min.)	150–160
Respiration Rate (per min.)	110–150
Breeding Season	Continuous
Gestation Period	60–72 days
Oestrus Cycle	16–19 days
Female No. Teats	Two
Earliest Recommended Breeding Age:	
Male	12–16 weeks
Female	5 months
Upper Breeding Age (average)	
Male	4–5 years
Female	3–4 years
Litter Size (average)	1–4
State of Young at Birth	Precocial
Weaning Age	21–30 days
Diet & Essential Vitamins	Herbivorous: C
Minimum Hutch Area	
For Single Animal	1860 sq. cm (2 sq. ft)
Number of Varieties (approx.)	30+